The What **Works**
The **Best** Principle

By
Lyle Dukes
and
Deborah Dukes

The biblical principle of hearing and yielding to God

The What Works The Best Principle -
The Biblical principle of hearing and yielding to God
Copyright © 2003

By Lyle Dukes and Deborah Dukes

All scripture quotations, unless otherwise noted, are from the Holy Bible, King James Version.

ISBN 1-888918-02-0

Lyle and Deborah Dukes Ministries
P.O. Box 431
Woodbridge, Virginia 22194

Harvest Word Publishing, Inc.
P.O. Box 4514
Woodbridge, Virginia 22194

First Printing March 2003, Second Printing February 2004
Printed in the United States of America

Cover designed by Tamara Jones

The What Works the Best Principle

Table of Contents

The What Works the Best Principle

Dedication

We would like to dedicate this book first and foremost to Our Lord and Savior Jesus Christ, who is the true author of *The What Works the Best Principle*. We have been tremendously blessed because of the perpetual presence of His Word.

We also dedicate this book to the powerful ministry couples that are dear to our hearts. To Bishop Carver and Co-Pastor Lorene Poindexter, Apostle Lawrence and Mother Gloria Campbell, Bishop Thomas D. and Mrs. Serita Jakes, Pastor John and Mrs. Diana Cherry, Bishop Alfred and Co-Pastor Susie Owens, Pastor John and Mrs. Trina Jenkins, Bishop Rufus and Mother Betty Hayes, Bishop McArthur and Mother Esther Anderson, Bishop Cornelius and Mother Augusta Showell, Pastor Bill and Mrs. Lynna Roberts, Pastors Robert and Shirley Burton, Pastor Roger and Mrs. Rosa Logan and others in ministry that have impacted our lives. You have influenced us, corrected us, inspired us and encouraged us. Thank you for teaching us, through word and deed, how to perform *What Works the Best*.

To the dedicated team of laborers: Jim Gillis, Lori Brooks, Shenell Shepard, Christine Mallory, Nichelle Gardner and Tamara Jones. Thank you for your technical skills, which were instrumental in bringing this manuscript to life.

Lyle and Deborah Dukes

The What Works the Best Principle

Foreword

One of the greatest things about serving God is knowing that He is our Father. We draw comfort from knowing that He is near. As a father, God desires the best for His children. He wants us to "prosper and be in health as our souls prosper," III John 2.

In order to bless us to become mature Christians, God presents a platform for us to employ our faith and develop our relationship with Him. Through the challenges and experiences of life, God deals with us concerning His Will. It is here that He seeks communication and trust from His children. *The What Works the Best Principle* is a concept based upon seeking, communicating, trusting and performing the Will of God.

Pastors Lyle and Deborah Dukes have presented, in this book, not just what it takes to be a better Christian, but better husbands and wives, fathers and mothers, supervisors and employees, teachers and students, pastors and leaders and so on.

The What Works the Best Principle can be applied to all facets of life. It deals with our humility before God and our trust to release the details of our lives into His hands. This book will challenge you to go to the next level and walk in the purpose that God has designed for your life.

Bishop Alfred A. Owens
Co-Pastor Susie C. Owens

The What Works the Best Principle

Introduction

People generally do not make sound decisions. In fact, if you took an honest look, you would see that mankind is very good at making bad choices. We do not know if we inherited it from our creative parents, Adam and Eve, who chose to do the only thing that God told them <u>not</u> to do (eating from the Tree of the Knowledge of Good and Evil) or if we have just developed bad judgment over time. But the fact remains, our track record on making sound decisions is not very good.

If we were good at decision-making we would see far fewer divorces, bankruptcies, foreclosures, and repossessions. There would be less adultery, prostitution, corporate crime in our boardrooms, alcoholism, and drug addiction. If we were just a little better at making decisions we would see a dramatic downward spiral in our crime rate! Some unfortunate situations may be attributed to uncontrollable events or misfortune, but the majority is just plain old bad decision-making.

We know that if things are left up to us, as mankind, we will soon fail. We expect and project this. We build new prisons before they are required because we know the propensity of mankind. We establish drug programs and detoxification centers for generations that have yet to try drugs. We hope for the best, expect the worst and plan assiduously for defeat. We expect and know that many in our society will make the wrong choices.

Many of our major health problems—heart attacks, lung disease, and diabetes to name a few, are overwhelmingly from bad choices or bad decision-making rather than from genetics, accidents or other reasons. The same is true for many of the ills of our society, which continue to ail us: teen pregnancy, illiteracy, and school violence.

We place such a very high value on decision-making that millions of dollars are spent annually looking into the background of individuals so we may feel comfortable with their ability to make the correct decisions. We scrutinize the records and resumes of those we would have lead us. The news media, along with other "watchdog" agencies, attempt to ensure that we are well informed about our political leaders, corporate giants, judges and others before they are elected or hired to positions of trust. We want to be assured that we have the people with the very best of character making decisions for us.

Time and time again we are faced with the results of bad decision-making. We simply do not take the paths that lead us to make good decisions. It would seem that our human nature fails us when we attempt to do so, but there is a solution. There is a better way. There is a process that ensures positive results and offers tremendous benefits for us as individuals in particular and mankind in general. It is based on something we call *The What Works The Best Principle.*

The What Works the Best Principle is a concept that is based on the Word of God. It is a principle steeped in the ways of individuals in the Bible who walked by faith and saw its results. They found out that, in performing the Will of God (or what works best), that God is "a rewarder of them that diligently seek Him."[1] The "seeking of truth" is the basis from which this principle is derived. It is based upon God's Word in order to produce better results. Since God is a God that cannot fail, we believe the quicker you get directions from God and perform them, the more successful you will become.

We have used *The What Works The Best Principle* for years. In the middle of family situations we say, "What is the best thing to do?" This puts us in a posture to hear from God. This principle has blessed our marriage, finances and careers. It has helped us in parenting and planning as well. It has helped us quickly assess situations while deflating emotions and fleshly attitudes such as pride and stubbornness. We continually say, "What is best in this situation?"—not what feels better or what looks better, but what is better. What is the Will of God? We have found that God rewards those that trust and seek Him in that fashion.

We catch a glimpse of our Lord Jesus Christ using this principle in the Garden of Gethsemane the night before He was to be judged, sentenced and crucified. As He prayed to God, He dealt with a complex array of emotions concerning His forthcoming plight. Jesus said, "Father, if thou be willing, remove this cup from me..."[2] At this point, it appears that Jesus wanted the suffering to end. He certainly had the

---

[1] Hebrews 11:6 But without faith it is impossible to please him: for he that cometh to God must believe that he is, and that he is a rewarder of them that diligently seek him.

[2] St. Luke 22:42 Saying, Father, if thou be willing, remove this cup from me: nevertheless not my will, but thine, be done.

"right" to be removed from the situation since he had not done anything wrong. However, Jesus continued to pray. His prayer took a dramatic turn when He said,

> "...nevertheless not my will, but thine, be done." [2]

He then chose to go to the cross and die.

What He chose to do did not feel better nor did it seem legally right (to take the life of an innocent man), but it was better because it was the Will of God! He had to die to redeem the millions of souls that would be covered by His blood and saved by His death. God gave instructions for what was best for that situation. Jesus denied the human "part" of himself so that the spiritual "part" would be glorified.

God wants to provide us His Will for every situation, decision, problem and crisis in our lives. With all the things that you can do, there is only one best thing to do. When used, this principle sequesters us into the presence of His Will and writes the calligraphy of the Word of God on the canvas of our souls. This process sits us at the feet of Jesus allowing Him to "download" directions for the next step in our life's journey.

Psalms 37:23 says:

> "The steps of a good man are ordered by the LORD:
> and he delighteth in his way."

---

[3] St. John 10:3-5: To him the porter openeth; and the sheep hear his voice: and he calleth his own sheep by name, and leadeth them out. 4 And when he putteth forth his own sheep, he goeth before them, and the sheep follow him: for they know his voice. 5 And a stranger will they not follow, but will flee from him: for they know not the voice of strangers.

14

When you continually say, "Lord, what is best?", "show me what to do," or "Give me the next step to take," you are prompting the Voice of the Lord. Asking this type of question opens the door for God to convey His Will for you. Jesus says that His sheep "…follow him: for they know his voice. And a stranger will they not follow,…"[3]

God desires that we live an abundant life. He wants us to prosper. He desires that we be in good health. Some of us are just surviving, not living. We fail at marriage because we have not learned how to have a blessed marriage. *The What Works the Best Principle* will lead you into having a blessed marriage. It will show you how to be blessed financially. These are God's desires. The scripture in III John 2 says,

"Beloved, I wish above all things that thou mayest prosper and be in health, even as thy soul prospereth."

He wants you to have an abundant life. He wants you to walk victoriously, receiving all the manifestations of His promises: That's God's heart.

The following chapters will further illustrate this principle.

The What Works
the Best Principle

Chapter One

You Are Just Winging It

Chances are that if you have reached a reasonable degree of success in your life, you probably do not know how you got there. Certainly, there are a few factors that stand out as monuments between the great seas of ambiguity that we like to attribute our success to such as a college education, military experience, taking over the family business or just plain old "hard work." However, this is <u>still</u> not enough to justify the magnitude of our success. There are people who have done these same things—and more—and have failed twice over.

If we were to really examine in detail the equation of our current status, it would probably be filled with things that simply do not "add up." If you made it through ten years of marriage, it is probably not because you followed a "manual to marital success." If you did not go to jail or did not try drugs, or once took drugs and now do not, it is probably due to something other than your moral fortitude.

So good or bad, or somewhere in between, how did we get here? How did we survive? What could have happened? Since there is no scientific formula or natural pattern to explain our personal phenomena we must look to the supernatural. We survived because of the grace and favor of God. Without His preserving power we could not have made it this far. Without His blessings we would not be prospering. Our contribution and the contributions of those around us are far less significant than the role He has played in our survival.

The reality is that we human beings have just been winging it. The majority of our choices are made without much thought, reason or information. We follow more trends, fads, and whims than we even realize. We are motivated by feelings and are moved more by circumstances than we are by mission. When something happens, we respond based on the level of impact and we shift our direction several degrees respectively. We are more like a fireman whose course is dictated by circumstances than a captain of a ship with a charted course.

We like to think we know where we are going and what we are doing, but the fact is we are just winging it. We spend a lot of time projecting an image of someone who has it all together—tough in character, confident in decisions, secure in spirit and happy in relationships. We try our best to personify someone who has a strong sense of direction and purpose, but in reality we have a hard time just picking out our clothes in the morning or selecting a restaurant for dinner. No matter what we project, we still are winging it.

Real security is found in the Lord Jesus Christ. We can be confident in Him because He will show us the way.

Proverbs 3:5-6 says:

> *"Trust in the LORD with all thine heart; and lean not unto thine own understanding. In all thy ways acknowledge him, and he shall direct thy paths."*

In Romans 8:28 we read:

> *"And we know that all things work together for good to them that love God, to them who are the called according to his purpose."*

In the realms of Christ we do not have to wing it anymore. God will set the stage and all we have to do is act out the script that He has given us. We can be confident in Christ and this confidence will breed competence.

As we examine *The What Works The Best Principle*, please understand that this principle relies on the fact that we as Christians yield to God and His plan for us. Trusting Him means that we do not have to wing it anymore. Oh, what a relief this is!

The What **Works** the **Best Principle**

Chapter Two

Do I Have A Choice?

Most Christians do not know it but they are serving a "life" sentence of self-incarceration. They are prisoners to their own limitations and fears, while bound by the chains of mediocrity and familiarity. As prisoners, they have lost hope of being anything beyond what they currently are. Somewhere behind the cold, self-erected walls of confinement they have misplaced their endeavors and aspirations of grandeur.

Satan comes and reinforces these cognitive walls by echoing the sentiment that "this is as good as it gets." He paints a dismal picture of "reality"—further fortifying the discouragement of the believer. His goal is to steal and kill their dreams, and ultimately destroy their destiny. Jesus said in St. John 10:10:

> *"The thief cometh not, but for to steal, and to kill, and to destroy:…"*

Prisoners do not generally think they have a choice in life-changing decisions. They believe that they must accept what "life" has given them. But there is good news—you are not a prisoner! If you have given your life to the Lord Jesus, then you are free!

You Do Have A Choice!

St. John 8:36 says:

> *"If the Son therefore shall make you free, ye shall be free indeed."*

This freedom gives you choices.

Believe it or not, success and failure can be traced back to choices. As we navigate through our complex and challenging lives, understand that the majority of results that we see have come directly from the choices that we have made.

Adam and Eve never reached their full potential because they chose to disobey God and eat from the Tree of the Knowledge of Good and Evil. Adam and Eve's son, Cain, made a series of bad choices which led to his judgment and nomadic lifestyle. But God presented choices to Cain even after his first bad choice.

Genesis 4:6-7 records this account:

> *"And the LORD said unto Cain, Why art thou wroth? and why is thy countenance fallen? If thou doest well,*

shalt thou not be accepted? and if thou doest not well, sin lieth at the door...."

It appears that after Cain had brought the wrong offering he could have returned and presented an "acceptable" offering. However, Cain chose to grow jealous and decided to kill his brother Abel who had done the right thing and presented the right kind of offering to God. The curse that was on Cain's life was the result of choice—it was clearly brought on by Cain himself.

You do not have to live under the bondage of a "bad decision" curse. If you do the right thing—in spite of the challenge to do wrong, inspired by the flesh, worldly influences and the devil himself, you will never face the consequences of that bad decision. If you have made a bad decision, start doing the right thing immediately! You may have to suffer through some of the judgment of that choice, but know that if you do the right thing you have started the process to reverse the curse. The Word of God declares:

> *"...no good thing will he withhold from them that walk uprightly."[4]*

Doing the right thing, as God has instructed, will bring very favorable results. In other words, if you choose to do right the majority of the time, like Abraham, Moses, Daniel or the prophets, you will see the results of what right choices bring. It is not that these men were right all of the time. These men were not right all of the time, however, they had a heart to do right which impacted their decision-making.

---

[4] Psalms 84:11 For the LORD God is a sun and shield: the LORD will give grace and glory: no good thing will he withhold from them that walk uprightly

At every stage in life, there are decisions to be made. You have the power to change the landscape of your horizon. If you are going to be financially blessed, debt-free or debt-filled, it is your choice. If your marriage is to be full and robust <u>or</u> limp and weak, it is your choice. If you are going to be an asset or a liability to God's Kingdom it is all up to you. It is your choice.

The What **Works** the **Best Principle**

Chapter Three

The Big Frustration

Are there times that you feel that you could just scream? The cacophony of unfulfilled destiny continues to daily reverberate throughout the corridors of your soul. There is a nagging thought that constantly comes up time and time again—"there must be something more to my life than just this." This frustration is understandable. Your spirit has great expectation but has seen little manifestation. Chances are you do not even know what "great thing" it is that you are going to do—but you know that this (your present state) cannot be it.

The reason you are frustrated is because you were designed for something significant. God has "fearfully and wonderfully" made you for a purpose. All of your skills, gifts, abilities and talents were given for that partifcular reason. All of that potential on "lock-down" inside you produces a friction between who you are and who you were designed to be. It is almost like a supersonic jet that never leaves the airport runway. It is full of fuel, has the power, is loaded with navigational gear and has a skillful, seasoned crew. However, it never leaves the ground. In order for it to takeoff, there is a series of things the crew must do—there is a "flight plan" that must be followed.

You are like that jet—you are ready for "takeoff" but there is a series of things that you must do. To follow your flight plan, you must come out of negative patterns and any sin or bondage that you might have in your life. You have to make up your mind to "unload the payload" and saturate yourself in Christ.

> *"Therefore if any man be in Christ, he is a new creature: old things are passed away; behold, all things are become new."* II Corinthians 5:17

Step-by-step you will get closer to where God wants you. You must be patient. Your course that God has designed is carefully choreographed to develop you at each stage. If you are sensitive enough to hear God's directions, He will guide you one step at a time. He provides directions from His Word:

> *"Thy word is a lamp unto my feet, and a light unto my path."* Psalms 119:105

Each step will be a choice that you will have to make. If you stay spiritually clear the choices will be obvious. You must ensure that you do not lose your focus concerning what God is doing and where He is taking you. It is easy to get discouraged when you look at where you are and your present circumstances. You must continue to focus on where you are going.

Do not get off track. You must constantly look at the "big picture." Do not be so quick to leave your church because you are not moving fast enough. Growth is a slow process. If you "uproot" you will have to be planted all over again. Do not be so quick to seek a divorce when things are not working well in your marriage or go out and spend on your credit card because it does not appear that your debt is moving. God must take you through some struggles so that you can be strengthened. View the frustrations that you have on the inside as a good thing. Turn the negative energy to positive. Use it as an indicator that lets you know you are not there yet, but you are on your way. By walking with the directions from the God who knows *what works the best*, you will reach your purpose and final destination in God.

The What **Works** the **Best Principle**

Chapter Four

Doing What Works the Best

We believe that the enemy sets up camp between our knowing and our doing the Will of God. Thus we will find an extreme challenge in performing *what works the best*. It is no secret to most of us that God's Word always provides the best solution to any problem or situation. We understand that within the framework of the Word of God are treasures of truth that will emphatically break the bondages of our past and the chains of our present to emancipate us into the freedom of our future.

> *"And ye shall know the truth, and the truth shall make you free."* St. John 8:32

We love to celebrate the testimonies of those that have embraced the Word of God and held on to see ultimate victory. We have even given scripture-based counsel to others on how to "overcome", but when it comes to performing the Word in our own lives—it becomes hard to do. It is strange how you can give sound instructions to everyone else, but cannot seem to obey the same set of instructions. It is time for us to cross the "great divide" from just hearing the Word of God to doing it.

Doing *What Works the Best* presents a tremendous challenge to our very nature. It would be easy if God's Will for us always agreed with our flesh—if His ways were just like our ways. This is seldom the case. In fact the scripture says in Isaiah 55:8:

> *"For my thoughts are not your thoughts, neither are your ways my ways, saith the LORD."*

So in order to get to God's plan, we must get out of <u>our</u> <u>way</u> and get into <u>His</u> <u>Way</u>. We must bypass the elaborate decision-making system that we have built within our minds—a system that is a product (or derivative) of our past experiences, fears, logical and analytical abilities, feelings and who knows what else. We must embrace by faith, the powerful and anointed plan that He has for our lives. This is an arduous process. It will by no means be easy. You must make up in your mind that you want change in your life and that you want to fulfill your purpose and destiny in God and then just do it! Break forth with a sedulous, tenacious spirit and bring forth the Will of God into your life.

Out of the lottery of choices that you have to deal with several times a day, you must be firm about employing this principle—and choose to do what is right in every case. This pattern of doing the Will of God will become a habitual process that will be installed in your thinking and lifestyle over time.

It is said that it takes about 30 days to form a habit. You should take the next 30 days to concentrate on doing *What Works the Best*. We believe that the reason most people do not get better, accomplish significant goals and are not blessed financially is because most people do not have focus. They aimlessly wander from day to day, week to week and let life happen to them. This process will make you take a look at every thing that you do and weigh it in the presence of the Lord. Each decision—now directed by the Lord Jesus Christ—becomes a step closer to the fulfillment of the purpose that God designed for you.

"The steps of a good man are ordered by the LORD: and he delighteth in his way." Psalms 37:23

In our 17 years of marriage, we can definitely see the benefits of focusing on *What Works the Best*. When we were first married, we thought that we had a good understanding of each other, because we had talked and spent time together for about five years. Furthermore, we had some good examples of marriages, as well as books and other resources. None of the above could have prepared us for what was to come. When two strong-willed people get together ultimately, those two must yield to God in order to do *What Works the Best*.

The personalities of people are so complex that there is really not one guide that will help them through. People need supernatural guidance from God. Spiritual counsel is good but you need more than that. After years of toil because of our love for each other, we committed to find a system that would help us through every problem and difficulty.

We continually heard the Word of God on a weekly and some times daily basis and as a result our hearts were open to hearing from God. We prayed and counseled with one another through tears and heart-to-heart discussions. As we humbled ourselves, God revealed to us this wonderful principle. It is nothing new. It is used by the people of God throughout the Bible—it just seemed to have no name. As we examined the lives of successful business owners, married couples and individuals, it finally hit us—something was going on that caused people to be successful. We were prompted to call it *The What Works The Best Principle*.

Employing this principle has blessed us in a wonderful way. We made a commitment not just to understand it but to perform it. We have been blessed by telling others about it. If you employ the principle you will surely see the results.

The What **Works** the **Best Principle**

Chapter Five

Deal With Your Flesh Quickly

Overcoming the desires of the flesh is probably the greatest problem that we face as believers. It is a continual struggle that we must endure. Since the flesh never leaves us—be assured that it will never leave us alone. If we escape the temptations of the flesh in one area, we can surely expect that they will surface in another. Your flesh will give you trouble. As long as we are living in our fleshly bodies in a world of temptation that is influenced by our adversary, Satan, we will have trouble. I John 2:16 says:

> *"For all that is in the world, the lust of the flesh, and the lust of the eyes, and the pride of life, is not of the Father but is of the world."*

The good news is that God gives us power to overcome through His Word. He always provides a way for us to be victorious. We must yield—

even though there are overwhelming temptations of the flesh—to God and to *What Works the Best*, which is His Word!

The scripture says in I Corinthians 10:13:

> *"There hath no temptation taken you but such as is common to man: but God is faithful, who will not suffer you to be tempted above that ye are able; but will with the temptation also make a way to escape, that ye may be able to bear it."*

As soon as you begin to employ *The What Works The Best Principle* within the framework of your daily walk, the flesh will meet you at the crossroads of change. It will try to "bully" you back into old patterns. It will do its best to run things. Do not let your flesh have its way. The flesh will try to "strong-arm" us in several ways. It will start with the areas where we have been the weakest. If you were an alcoholic, the flesh would say, "a drink is what you need." If you had a problem telling the truth, it would try to get you entangled in a lie. Whatever area you struggled in, that is the area in which the flesh will try to rise again.

To succeed in your struggle against temptation, you must take immediate action against the flesh. You must deal with the flesh quickly. You cannot allow the flesh to rise and saturate your thinking. Your decisions will be made based upon the "mainstream" thoughts that are flowing through your mind and, if they are carnal, the actions that follow will be carnal.

Pride

Pride is a common tool that the flesh uses <u>against</u> *The What Works the Best Principle*. A good example of this may be found in discussions between a husband and wife as to who will be primarily responsible for handling the finances for their home. It is not a difficult task to find out *What Works the Best*. If you pray, God will probably say whomever can do it best. If the husband is not good with numbers and did not finish high school and the wife is a certified public accountant (CPA) and very good administratively, then the answer is pretty clear. However, pride gets in the man and says, "You are the man; you should be in control of the money." Therein, you have a problem. Pride will blind the individual that possesses it. The husband cannot "see" why he should not be over the finances. This brings conflict and bad management to their home. Instead of going up, they spiral downward. This happens all because of pride.

Pride will also try to lock you into what we call the "I am not wrong" syndrome. This type of pride is developed when the individual believes that he is right all or the majority of the time. This belief is so strong that it hinders normal hearing. It prohibits the entertaining of logic or reasoning and the individual will not understand simple concepts. During a period of reasoning, those with this kind of problem will spout out phrases such as, "That's your opinion" and "I am not usually wrong."

People that suffer from pride of the "I am not wrong" syndrome are blind to the truth. Because they are intoxicated by their need to be right—they seldom see *What Works the Best*. These individuals are easily identified, even by casual observers, because they have the propensity to be so off-base. They stick out like a sore thumb. When the best solution is finally revealed, individuals with this type of prideful spirit will claim that this was the same thing they were saying—just presented a little differently. Even if they had a strong position opposite of the best solution—they will try to make the switch just to be right.

People plagued by this syndrome will constantly cover themselves. There is nothing negative about saying, "I was wrong," but they seem to have a problem saying it. They are constantly stealing the thunder of other people's original ideas by saying, "I was thinking of that." While working, they camouflage their inability and lack of attention with the after-the-fact phrase, "I was going to do that." Individuals with this "runaway" pride are difficult to work with, will never be team players, and are down right sickening to be around. Since you have to make so many concessions for them and expend so much energy working around them, it is hard to maintain a positive and progressive working environment when they are present.

> *"Pride goeth before destruction, and an haughty spirit before a fall."* Proverbs 16:18

I Peter 5:6 says:

> *"Humble yourselves therefore under the mighty hand of God, that he may exalt you in due time:"*

When pride arises, you must deal with it. Since it negates the influence of the Holy Spirit, it must be dealt with very quickly. You must reach beyond your flesh and say, "What is really best for this situation?"

Stubbornness

Stubbornness is another major flesh "blocker" of *What Works the Best*. It is knowing the truth but not obeying it—understanding the Will of God but not yielding to it. In the 25th chapter of I Samuel, the Bible describes a stubborn man by the name of Nabal. The scripture (I Samuel 25:3) depicts this man as being "churlish and evil in all his doings." The word, "churlish" means stubborn, stiff-necked or hard-hearted. His wife Abigail, on the other hand, is characterized as being "a woman of good understanding and of a beautiful countenance."

In this story God illuminates the dangers of being stubborn and how it can cause us to miss out on the great things of God. In this passage of scripture, David and his small army of about six hundred men had dwelt in Carmel. While there, they came upon the servants of Nabal along with some of Nabal's great possessions (he had three thousand sheep and a thousand goats). David, while not yet king, but still very famous, protected Nabal's personnel and business from thieves for an extended period of time at no charge. I Samuel states that during that period when David was with Nabal's servants they did not lose any of their possessions. At a certain point, David decided to send out ten young men in peace to the house of Nabal to request food for himself and his men. Nabal, knowing full well the deeds of David and what he should do as a courtesy for their labor, responded in pure stubbornness. He said to David's men in I Samuel 25:10-11:

> *"...Who is David? and who is the Son of Jesse? there be many servants now a days that break away every man from his master. Shall I then take my bread, and my water, and my flesh that I have killed for my*

shearers, and give it unto men, whom I know not whence they be?"

David was angry when he received this report. He gathered and equipped four hundred men in full battle attire to go down and destroy the house of Nabal. About that same time, some of the servants of Nabal who overheard Nabal's conversation with David's men told Abigail what had transpired.

It is interesting that the servants understood that they could not reason with Nabal because (1 Samuel 25:17) "he is such a son of Belial that <u>a man cannot speak to him</u>."[5] Belial was a wicked thinking or ungodly tribe of people. Abigail gathered a peace offering of food and met David and his army before they reached the house of Nabal and pleaded for forgiveness. David had a change of heart because of her wisdom. She did what worked the best! She later had a feast for David and his men, and Nabal was so drunk that he did not even notice the reason for the celebration. When he sobered up the next morning, Abigail told him everything that had happened—literally how she had saved their lives and salvaged their business, but Nabal did not rejoice. Due to his stubbornness, the Bible says his "heart died within him and he became as a stone." He died about ten days later—all because of stubbornness.

Please do not let pride blind you or stubbornness destroy you. Do not allow your hearing to be blocked because of the works of the flesh. When your flesh arises, deal with it immediately! Confront your

---

[5] I Samuel 25:17 Now therefore know and consider what thou wilt do; for evil is determined against our master, and against all his household: for he is such a son of Belial, that a man cannot speak to him.

flesh and change your mind. Tell yourself, "I am not going to let my flesh have its way. I <u>will</u> do *What Works the Best.*"

Pride and stubbornness are certainly strong influences of the flesh but there are many others. It could be fear that paralyzes your progress, or anger and bitterness that shuts the gate on the Will of God. It may be past hurts or insecurities that stymie your steps or complaining and negative talk that keep you in the barrenness of the desert. But whatever it is that tries to work through your flesh—you must move quickly and deal with it—address it through obedience to the Word of God. Yield yourself to *What Works the Best.*

The What Works the Best Principle

Chapter Six

Acknowledge When You Are Wrong

One of the most effective means to keep yourself in a posture to receive *What Works the Best* from God is to acknowledge when you are wrong. It is no secret that we (human beings) are often wrong. Openly addressing our faults and confessing our sins helps us to concede our will to God's Will. When we admit our transgressions we actually change the spiritual landscape and ambience that abides within us. As we continually address our issues, the examination alone causes us to understand that we really do not know what we are doing and that we certainly need God to show us the way.

Most people have casually identified times when they were wrong but because they have "looked the other way" and did not address the painful details of their infraction, they ended up with the feeling that maybe they were not so wrong. With just a cursory understanding of their problem, they hindered their opportunity for growth. This clandestine debilitating condition clogs our spiritual arteries, prevents the flow of truth and thus pushes us away from the presence of the Lord. Our relationships, finances, career progression, day-to-day activities and dreams are all thwarted when we do not acknowledge that we are wrong. This even hinders our relationship with God. God told the Children of Israel in Hosea 5:15[6]:

> *"I will go and return to my place, till they acknowledge their offence, and seek my face:..."*

I John 1:9-10 states:

> *"If we confess our sins, he is faithful and just to forgive us our sins, and to cleanse us from all unrighteousness. If we say that we have not sinned, we make him a liar, and his word is not in us."*

We need to get into a consistent pattern of confession. Owning up to our wrongdoing affords us the opportunity to draw closer to God. Recognizing our offenses is the first step to truth. This must be followed up with repentance and commitment. With these spiritually progressive entities in place, we will be well on our way to spiritual health.

James 5:16[7] tells us to:

> *"Confess your faults one to another, and pray one for another that ye may be healed...."*

---

[6] Hosea 5:15 I will go and return to my place, till they acknowledge their offence, and seek my face: in their affliction they will seek me early.

[7] James 5:16 Confess your faults one to another, and pray one for another, that ye may healed. The effectual fervent prayer of a righteous man availeth much.

Actively and verbally "publicizing" that you are wrong ushers in a wonderful spirit of humility which is a great "pride fighter." It also opens your eyes to see *What Works the Best*. If you never get over the unpleasant distress of being wrong, then you can never really embrace the plan that God has to make it right.

Jesus said in St. Matthew 23:12:

> *"And whosoever shalt exalt himself shall be abased; and he that shall humble himself shall be exalted."*

Humble yourself, acknowledge your faults and receive *What Works the Best*.

The What Works the Best Principle

Chapter Seven

Living For The Long Run

Most of us have done some real foolish things in our lives. Many of these infractions were probably ill-advised or due to short-sightedness. When we think on these past things, we wish we had a chance to do them over again. We cannot. But, if possible we would certainly do things differently. We would approach the same situation in a more mature manner.

Maturity is seeing the "big picture." It is understanding that what we do now will affect what is up ahead. It is the ability to see past our present circumstances and ascertain the overall effect that our actions may have.

Mature Christians are living for the long run. They want to achieve the best possible result so that they may please God. Walking by faith includes humbling yourself so that you are not "caught up" in the moment.

"Humble yourselves therefore under the mighty hand of God, that he may exalt you in due time:"
I Peter 5:6

It is not about what I want but what God wants for my life, for He knows what is best.

Seasons of Life

There are seasons in our lives just as there are seasons on the Earth. Each season brings with it particular characteristics. It will not seem clear until you have had a few years under your belt but everyone has seasons. There will be some winters where there is seemingly no growth. There is nothing new on the horizon, friends may be few and difficulties come like a winter storm without warning. There will be some spring seasons where newness and growth are obvious. It is a season with new opportunities and aspirations blown in on the winds of change. There will be summer seasons where you can enjoy the fruit of the springtime and congenial activities of relationships while enduring the sweltering heat of challenge in other areas of your life. There will be autumns when the once new becomes old like brown leaves on a tree and things that were very stable begin to fall off and blow away. There will be seasons in our lives.

As we live for the long run, we must understand that we will see many seasons in our lifetime. For that reason it is important to know that these seasons will come and go. Every season has a beginning and an end. Herein lies the reason and need for spiritual maturity. Maturity helps us connect with the big picture, instead of being focused on a particular season and what it brings. Young children have a hard time understanding seasons. You have to remind them at times, that the season will change from winter to spring—that soon it will be warm again.

The Best Is Yet To Come

The What Works the Best Principle is a means to an end. It is the employment of a process that is designed to optimize your standard of living while ultimately propelling you closer to the destination that God has designated for your life. Living for the "long run" is knowing that no matter what you face—good, bad or otherwise, if you continue to perform God's Will, it will work out for the best.

Romans 8:28 says:

> *"And we know that all things work together for good to them that love God, to them who are the called according to his purpose."*

Understand that the best is yet to come. We will fulfill tremendous things right here on Earth through our faithfulness to God, and at the close of this life we will be translated into a greater life— eternal life with our Lord Jesus Christ. Truly the best is yet to come!

The What Works
the Best Principle

Chapter Eight

Letting Go Of Your Understanding

"Trust in the LORD with all thine heart; and lean not unto thine own understanding. In all thy ways acknowledge him, and he shall direct thy paths." Proverbs 3:5-6

In order to sincerely embrace God's best for you, you must release your preconceived notions of what you think is best for you. This is probably one of the most difficult things to do. Because we are creatures of habit we have, for years, entrenched ourselves in our current routines and patterns. Therefore, we have developed an elaborate, complicated machine (in our minds) that figures out what is best. This "machine" churns out an answer whether it makes sense or not. Some things that we do are senseless, harmful or destructive. But because they are a part of our "make up," we draw a sense of security from their familiarity.

Most of us do not have an active campaign to eliminate the vices in our lives. Furthermore, there probably is no real strategy for installing and deploying virtuous qualities.

The reason that we do not get better or seek positive change is because we think that we are all right. We really think that we "got it going on." Even with our insecurities, fits of depression and continual failures, somewhere in the recesses of our mind, we still think that we have it together.

> *"There is a way that seemeth right unto a man, but the end thereof are the ways of death." Proverbs 16:25*

As long as we think we know the way, we cannot get any help from God. We cannot trust the Lord and lean to our own understanding at the same time. When we let go of what we know, God promises in Proverbs 3:6[8] to direct our paths with *What Works the Best*.

St. John 14:6 reads:

> *"Jesus saith unto him, I am the way, the truth, and the life: no man cometh unto the Father, but by me."*

Letting go is the first real challenge that most of us have. It tells us to give up our current belief structure and replace it with our trust in God. Letting go requires us to close down a very tangible humanistic way, with data, experiences, visual pictures of the past and logic. We must begin to operate in the intangible—believing God by faith.

---

[8] Proverbs 3:6 In all thy ways acknowledge him, and he shall direct thy paths.

"For we walk by faith, not by sight:"
II Corinthians 5:7

This is rather difficult because we have "sight." We possess a detailed analysis and assessment of the situation that we are currently going through. To lean to our own understanding means that we cognitively have an idea of what to do—we "see" it. Our mind gives us the best course of action. This happens automatically. To let go means that we have <u>an</u> answer already but we must release it so that we may obtain <u>the</u> answer. Thus, we must surrender what we have to *What Works the Best*, which is the Will of God.

Letting go of what you know challenges the intrinsic nature of your very being. In order to receive what is best from God we must get into a habit of releasing. This requires changing the way you think, not just putting a new process in place. Every time there is a decision to be made or some challenge presents itself, you must automatically yield to the mind of Christ.

Philippians 2:5 says:

> *"Let this mind be in you, which was also in Christ Jesus:"*

Romans 12:1-2 states for us to:

> *"...present your bodies a living sacrifice, holy, acceptable unto God, which is your reasonable service. And be not conformed to this world: but be ye transformed by the renewing of your mind, that ye may*

prove what is that good, and acceptable, and perfect, will of God."

As we set our minds to do God's Will, we will see the power of God manifested in our lives. It all starts with letting go of our understanding.

The What Works the Best Principle

Chapter Nine

Know Your Spiritual Strength

We believe that it is important to know where you are in terms of your present spiritual environment. It is necessary to have a good understanding of your personal spiritual strength. Someone may say, "I have been saved for several years, coming to church, praying, reading the scripture—where do I stand in the Lord? How strong am I really?" The truth is you are not as strong as you probably think you are. Do not misunderstand what we are saying—all those things are good and necessary for your spiritual growth. You are, however, only as strong as your current connection to the power source.

It is like asking a light bulb, "How bright can you shine? What is your electrical strength?" Even a light bulb in perfect working condition—brand new off the shelf—will only shine to the extent of the electricity coming from the power source. It is powerful as long as it is connected and the switch is turned on. When there is a disconnection, there is no power.

We do a lot of work "perfecting" ourselves—and we should (we should stop drinking, smoking, lying, being stubborn, etc.), but that in itself does not give us power. The power to be victorious comes exclusively from our Lord Jesus Christ. The scripture says in I John 4:4:

> *"...greater is he that is in you, than he that is in the world."*[9]

In essence, to be victorious we must link to the power source. There is no real spiritual power in us as natural beings. We have seen people who try to get their lives together without God. They say they are "turning over a new leaf." They make a good effort at rearranging their lives—but that is all that it is, a rearrangement. It is the kind of thing that you do in your living room. You move the sofa, tables and lamps and you call it a change. It is not really a change. It is a rearrangement. Change is moving into a brand new house with brand new furniture. Only God has the power to bring real change into your life. With God, you will have the strength to move forward.

David understood the source of his power when he, according to I Samuel 17:17, was tasked to take lunch to his brothers on the front line as the armies of Israel and the Philistines prepared to do battle. He noticed that there was no forward progress because of the Philistines' weapon of mass destruction—a giant named Goliath. David immediately reached for the power of God through his faith. He knew if this giant were to be defeated, it would not be because of the army's fighting ability, or his personal combat skills, but the Power of God.

---

[9] I John 4:4 Ye are of God, little children, and have overcome them: because greater is he that is in you, than he that is in the world.

Paul warns man in Romans 12:3[10] "...not to think of himself more highly than he ought to think;..." When confronted with situations, we have the tendency to think that we can handle them. We think that through our charisma, skills and abilities we can work them out. Beware of your personal pride—lest you fall.[11] God longs for us to trust Him.

Again, Proverbs 3:5 says:

"Trust in the LORD ..."

David recognized that his strength was limited so he trusted in his God whose power is unlimited. He trusted in a God who had the power to get the job done! He stated in I Samuel 17:45[12], "...Thou comest to me with a sword and with a spear and with a shield but I come to thee in the name of the Lord..." David defeated his giant. Are there giants in your life that need to be defeated? Are there mountains in your way that need to be removed? God has the strength to do it.

When the disciples came back to Jesus after a tremendous ministry experience, they were excited because they were able to work miracles. They exclaimed:

"...LORD, even the devils are subject unto us through thy name."[13]

[10] Romans 12:3 For I say, through the grace given unto me, to every man that is among you, not to think of himself more highly than he ought to think; but to think soberly, according as God hath dealt to every man the measure of faith.

[11] I Corinthians 10:12 Wherefore let him that thinketh he standeth take heed lest he fall.

[12] I Samuel 17:45 Then said David to the Philistine, Thou comest to me with a sword, and with a spear, and with a shield: but I come to thee in the name of the LORD of hosts, the God of the armies of Israel, whom thou hast defied.

[13] St. Luke 10:17 And the seventy returned again with joy, saying, Lord, even the devils are subject unto us through thy name.

However, Jesus stated in St. Luke 10:20[14]:

> *"...rejoice not, that the spirits are subject unto you; but rather rejoice, because your names are written in heaven."*

Jesus wanted them to understand that the power was not really theirs to rejoice over. The power came from God and God used the disciples as a conduit of that power. He wanted them to focus on the fact that they were "positionally postured" to receive that power—that is what He wanted them to rejoice over! Are you positionally postured to receive power from God?

Get The Hook Up

You may ask, "How can I get this power to be resident in my life?" "How can I have access to the kind of strength to perform *What Works the Best?*" This is done by (1) recognizing that you have no power, (2) knowing that God is your source of power and (3) making a conscious effort to yield to God's process so that a spiritual transaction may take place. This transaction will take place at the point that you intentionally and sincerely yield to God. The scripture says:

> *"Humble yourselves therefore under the mighty hand of God, that he may exalt you in due time."*
> I Peter 5:6

---

[14] St. Luke 10:20 Notwithstanding in this rejoice not, that the spirits are subject unto you; but rather rejoice, because your names are written in heaven.

Humility is the key. Humility says "God, I do not know what to do—and if I did, I do not have the power to bring it to pass." Humility is relying on God.

Hebrews 11:6 says:

> *"But without faith it is impossible to please him: for he that cometh to God must believe that he is, and that he is a <u>rewarder of them that diligently seek him</u>."*
> *(emphasis added)*

God rewards those that believe and seek Him. Believing and seeking is a good definition for worship. God is looking for worshipers to work through. In St. John 4:14[15] Jesus told the woman at the well:

> *"...but the water that I shall give him shall be in him a well of water springing up into everlasting life."*

Wells were necessities in the Middle Eastern culture during the time of Jesus. When settlers found a potential area to set up camp, one of the first things that they would do was dig a well. If there was no water they would have to move on. It was a necessary resource. Jesus stated that he wanted to put a well in us. He wanted his children to be a resource for others. People in your present environment will change because they will receive from the well that God puts in you. Furthermore, God will be the source for the resource!

---

[15] St. John 4:14 But whosoever drinketh of the water that I shall give him shall never thirst; but the water that I shall give him shall be in him a well of water springing up into everlasting life.

If you humble yourself, God will "hook" you up with power. As the power flows through you to be a resource for others—it will ultimately be a very present resource for you! Our God is an awesome God!

The What **Works** **the Best Principle**

Chapter Ten

Training Your Spirit

Implementing *The What Works The Best Principle* may <u>not</u> be as easy as it sounds. It is not a skill that most will acquire overnight. In order to install this concept on the "hard drive" of your souls, you must overthrow existing patterns, break through old mindsets and employ a shifting of your very paradigm. In order to be in a position where you are consistently seeking and performing *"The What Works The Best Principle,"* you must train your spirit. If you are ever going to bring the reality and fullness of God's Will into your life—there must be a personal revolution.

We see this challenge for change as a "spiritual boot camp." When a young man or woman goes to military boot camp or basic training, they are made to deal with, in detail, the person that they are. They have the opportunity to see first hand, their strengths and weaknesses, skills and flaws, self esteem and insecurities and so on. Some do not know how to make their bed, clean up or deal with people.

They may not have noticed these things before, but the boot camp environment intentionally brings them out.

Basic training also provides good, hard, regimented training to develop and perfect the skills that are not present. In order to be the persons that they are to become, training or "positive conflict" must occur. Daily, the drill sergeant drives these potential soldiers past what they want to do into a military mindset—to what a soldier would do. In the process, they learn to be obedient to orders, loyal to their country and fearless in combat.

This "driving" is what must occur to employ a new pattern or concept into your life. Training your spirit is not just reading a book or praying that something happens, but it is experiencing the positive conflict that is presented by the Word of God as it goes against your flesh. It is the militant process of overcoming the old man and all of his thoughts, ways, faults, idiosyncrasies, habits and sins and replacing them with the new regime—the new man and God's Will.

Truth Seekers Mentality

Part of the training process will be to develop a "truth seekers mentality." Most of us are not truth seekers although we like to think that we are. It sounds good when we say, "I live by the truth of God's Word." But what does that really mean? It simply means that we want what God wants. His Will is valid and our will is void. We know that God's truth will make us free, but freedom always has a price. When you seek truth, at some point, God will require you to sacrifice. While you seek truth, understand that your plans will not always agree with His plans. You will give when you thought you could keep, you will lose when you thought you would gain, and you must sever relationships that you do not want to let go of. You will, seemingly, give up the right for the wrong. The natural man wants fairness but God's Will and what works best will not seem fair.

A truth seeker's mentality starts with understanding that the truth may hurt. There may be some crucifixion along the way but the truth seeker knows that without a reviling crucifixion, there cannot be a glorious resurrection.

Ask, Seek, Knock

A truth seeker is always asking, seeking and knocking. Jesus said in St. Luke 11:9:

> *"And I say unto you, Ask, and it shall be given you; seek, and ye shall find; knock, and it shall be opened unto you."*

You must train yourself to be an active seeker of truth, a person that is always trying to live and do right before God. As each challenge presents itself, the truth seeker continually develops his spirit to desire the need for truth—for *What Works the Best*. As each issue, circumstance or situation is dealt with, the seeker embraces God's Will—in spite of the temptation of the flesh (pride, stubbornness, revenge, etc.), the world and the devil.

This can only be successful if you continually ask, seek and knock. Asking automatically causes you to question whether you have the best answer. You must train your spirit to do this. When a problem arises—so should the questions—"God, what is Your solution for this problem?" and "What is best in this situation?" If you never seek God for the answer, then you will do what you "feel" or what the flesh wants by default. Many of us have been in trouble because we did not consult God first. We have usually asked the questions after the damage has already been done.

Seeking deals with continual searching for information after you have asked. You must not just "ask" and forget about it. Train your spirit to seek out more details from God concerning the situation. Most problems that we face are pretty complex. We need further instructions and they are obtained through seeking. The word "seek" moves us past casual asking. It means staying there and "digging" until we get the directions that we need to carry out God's Will. If we seek, God promised that we would find. When we were children we used to go on Easter Egg hunts. What we wanted (the egg) was never just right there in front of us—but with some seeking—we would find our eggs. God wants us to get into the habit of seeking Him and His Will for our lives.

Knocking is another level of asking and seeking. It is being relentless about *What Works the Best*. It is obtaining a sedulous spirit that is settled and reserved just for the Will of God. Throughout the 15 chapters of St. Luke and in this particular passage, Jesus described our need to have this ask, seek, knock (for truth) mentality engrained in our spirit. Notice how each level intensifies: ask, seek, knock. God want us to be passionate about His truth!

Train your spirit to continually ask *"What Works the Best?"* Keep verbally, consciously saying it until it becomes a part of your subconscious. Train your spirit not to look at the peripherals that the circumstances bring (hurt feelings and embarrassment, etc.), but what God wants. Training your spirit will be challenging but well worth it in the long run.

The What **Works** the **Best Principle**

Chapter Eleven

Be Open To God

One of the wonderful things that we have found out about God is that He is always looking to give us instructions concerning what we are to do and directions for where we ought to go. Our wonderful marriages, exciting careers and the tremendous experiences that we have enjoyed along the way are unequivocally due to hearing and being obedient to the Voice of God. We feel therefore, that it is imperative to maintain an "always open" disposition with God—"Lord, I am always open to hear what you want to tell me, always open to do what you want me to do, always open to say what you want me to say," and so on.

This approach will always keep you "on-line" with God in a temperament to receive the next "download" of what is best for your life. You must pursue a listening spirit. Whatever situations you are in—good, bad or indifferent, seek to hear the expressed utterance of God. In the Book of Revelation, Jesus proclaimed several times:

"He that hath an ear, let him hear what the Spirit saith unto the churches;..." Revelation 2:11

Listening for God is tough, especially when there is a lot of "talk" going on. In this information age, there is no shortage of opinion, counsel, guidance, advice columns, mentoring, coaching, teaching, or recommendations. There is something to say on everything and several ways to say it. Through the cacophony of voices it is important that we discern the voice of God.

This is done through a personal and prolific prayer connection with God. Prayer, supplication and a continual seeking God's presence ensures that the heavenly lines are connected and clear. While prayer can be done on your knees in your "secret closet", it is not limited to this posture. After you get off your knees, the "prayer wheels" should still be turning so God can continue to minister to you and through you throughout the rest of the day.

"...The effectual fervent prayer of a righteous man availeth much." James 5:16

With an open line to God, you can continually take advantage of The *What Works the Best Principle*. Whatever you do, keep that line open. Do not allow yourself to be locked into seeing things one way. Push yourself beyond the limitations of your flesh and hear the Voice of God.

Beware Of Flesh Traps

As you pursue God's presence through your open line of communication with Him, please beware of the "flesh traps" that the enemy will set through pride and a haughty spirit. When you pray on a consistent basis and walk upright before God, you will move through the corridors of spiritual growth into the higher echelons of the things of God. When this happens, you are subject to the same kind of temptations that Lucifer, the son of the morning and high-level angel, was subject to. He ultimately was cast down (Isaiah 14)[16] and we know him now as Satan, the devil.

Do not misunderstand us, you should want to be as spiritual as possible, but do not lose your humility before God. Many people, when they cross the threshold into greater levels, unknowingly lose their spirituality and slip into a fabricated humanistic spirituality. We can be "spiritual" without God—just check out the praise and worship going on at your hometown professional football or basketball game. We can do this because God blew into Adam, our father, the spirit or "breath of life." However, this is not a God connection. There are many people that go from church to church, convention to convention and place to place but are out of the Will of God. They are not obedient and are constantly out of order, yet they want to give you a prophecy or preach to you the Word of God. Some of these folks are in continual sin. They may have once been "anointed" (or approved by God), but now they clearly are not. Beware of flesh traps!

---

[16] Isaiah 14:12 How art thou fallen from heaven, O Lucifer, son of the morning! how are thou cut down to the ground, which didst weaken the nations!

God Said

An open connection and dialogue with God comes with some warning. Be careful not to misuse this blessed privilege that God has established. The main purpose of God talking to you is to help you get better. You will ultimately help others through this gift but understand that God wants to speak to you. Many people get excited about their new "open line" with God and begin to use very casually, "God said…" Pretty soon it filters into their daily conversation and they begin to attribute many things to God that He did not say. This is a serious error. We believe that it is better not to use the phrase, "God said" at all than to be wrong about what God has said. If He said it, you do not have to mention that He said it for it to come to pass.

Some people use the phrase to manipulate others. For example, they may say, "God told me to tell you to give me $100." Most young Christians will not question the source because they want to be obedient to God. Others use "God said" or "the Spirit told me" so they will not be questioned concerning their motives. They will say, "God told me not to come to church last Sunday." Instead of dealing with the problem of laziness or sin, they officially chalk it up as some spiritual experience. When someone tells us God told them to do something we usually do not question them—and we are pastors. Jesus said in St. Matthew 5:37:

> *"But let your communication be, Yea, yea; Nay, nay:*
> *for whatsoever is more than these cometh of evil."*

If you keep your spiritual line connected and clear, then you will surely experience *What Works the Best* from God.

The What **Works** the **Best Principle**

Chapter Twelve

Stay With It

"And let us not be weary in well doing: for in due season we shall reap, if we faint not." Galatians 6:9

In order to ensure that the Will of God is incessantly and perpetually present in your life, you must work at it. We know that God will never "leave us or forsake us" (Hebrews 13:5)[17] but there will still be the constant challenges of the flesh, the world and Satanic influences. If we maintain our spiritual equanimity in God and continue to do right each step of the way, God promises to give us His best. Psalms 84:11[18] says:

> *"...no good thing will he withheld from them that walk uprightly."*

---

[17] Hebrews 13:5 Let your conversation be without covetousness; and be content with such things as ye have: for he hath said, I will never leave thee, nor forsake thee.

[18] Psalms 84:11 For the LORD God is a sun and shield: the LORD will give grace and glory: no good thing will he withhold from them that walk uprightly.

However, remember that reaping time will take place after sowing and growing time. *The What Works the Best Principle* needs to be employed at all times. You must consistently push this principle into the forefront of your spirit. Always ask yourself the question, "What works the best?" With this tenacity you will fulfill your purpose in God, but, you must stay with it.

You must be committed to the process. If you give up, you will forfeit the next stages of power and anointing that God has for your life. If you throw in the towel, you may have to go back and do old works again to get back up. Keep moving forward. There will be times when the road will be rough—but keep walking. Give yourself a "gut" check every now and then by asking—"Am I doing what works best?" As you move forward through the struggles of life God will continue to develop your character.

II Timothy 2:3 says:

> *"Thou therefore endure hardness, as a good soldier of Jesus Christ."*

Understand that *The What Works The Best Principle* is a tremendous tool for the believer, but it will only work if you continue to use it. You cannot apply this principle once or twice and expect to reap great benefits. Set it in motion and stay with it. In the weeks, months and years to come you will see the great benefit of aggressively and diligently seeking the Will of God for your life. As you weigh every decision, aspiration, motive and detail of your life in the balances of God, you will ultimately reap a life of blessings that is pleasing to God.

"But without faith it is impossible to please him: for he that cometh to God must believe that he is, and that he is a rewarder of them that diligently seek him."
Hebrews 11:6

The What Works the Best Principle

Epilogue

We See Jesus

Hebrews 2:3-9 *3 "How shall we escape, if we neglect <u>so great salvation;</u> which at the first began to be spoken by the Lord, and was confirmed unto us by them that heard him; 4 God also bearing them witness, both with signs and wonders, and with divers miracles, and gifts of the Holy Ghost, according to his own will? 5 For unto the angels hath he not put in subjection the world to come, whereof we speak. 6 But one in a certain place testified, saying, What is man, that thou art mindful of him? Or the son of man, that thou visitest him? 7 Thou madest him a little lower than the angels; thou crownedst him with glory and honour, and didst set him over the works of thy hands: 8 Thou hast put all things in subjection under his feet. For in that he put all in subjection under him, he left nothing that is not put under him. But now we see not yet all things put under him. 9 <u>But we see Jesus,</u> who was made a little lower than the angels for the suffering of death, crowned with glory and honour; that he by the grace of God should taste death for every man."*

As we seek God's best for us, we must not overlook "so great salvation." If we are really seekers of truth, we will find just what God wants us to find – a personal relationship with Him. In our enduring effort to please God, it is important to understand that our ultimate success starts with salvation through Jesus Christ. In fact, there is no real life without salvation. Jesus tells us in St. John 14:6 that He is "the way, the truth and the life."

When we look back at how we were living destructive lives, but we were preserved by a force that was totally beyond us – we see Jesus. If we understand that suicide should have cut our lives short, but God kept us by His grace – we see Jesus. He is really *What Works the Best* for our lives.

The What Works the Best Principle

Scriptural References

1. III John 2
2. Hebrews 11:6
3. St. Luke 22:42
4. Psalms 37.23
5. St. John 10:3
6. Proverbs 3:5-6
7. Romans 8:28
8. St. John 10:10
9. St. John 8:36
10. Genesis 4:6-7
11. Psalms 84:11
12. II Corinthians 5:17
13. Psalms 119:105
14. St. John 8:32
15. Isaiah 55:8
16. I Peter 5:6
17. Proverbs 16:25
18. St. John 14:6
19. II Corinthians 5:7
20. Philippians 2:5
21. Romans 12:1
22. I John 4:4
23. I Samuel 17:17
24. Roman 12:3
25. I Samuel 17:45
26. St. Luke 10:17
27. I Corinthians 10:12
28. St. Luke 10:20
29. St. John 4:14
30. St. Luke 11:931.
31. I John 2:16
32. I Corinthians 10:13
33. Proverbs 16:18
34. I Samuel 25
35. Hosea 5:15
36. I John 1:9-10
37. James 5:16
38. St. Matthew 23:13
39. Revelations 2:11
40. St. Matthew 5:37
41. Galatians 6:9
42. Hebrews 13:5
43. Psalms 84:11
44. II Timothy 2:3

About Pastor Lyle Dukes and Co-Pastor Deborah Dukes and Harvest Life Changers Church, International

Pastor and Co-Pastor Dukes have been commissioned by God to reach the world and change lives through the preaching and teaching of God's Word. It is their desire to see every believer broken free from the chains of bondage and walking progressively in the manifestation of God's promises.

Over the past seven years, Harvest has become a life-changing place of growth and deliverance through the power of Jesus Christ. God has continued to send souls to hear these anointed and appointed vessels. Today, the church has over two thousand members and countless visitors who come to worship God, be saved, delivered and set free.

If you are ever in the Woodbridge, Virginia area, we invite you to worship with us on Sundays at 8:00 a.m., 9:00 a.m. and 11:30 a.m. and on Wednesdays for Pastoral Bible Teaching at 7:30 p.m.

For additional information, you may call (877) 867-3853 or visit www.harvestlifechangers.com.

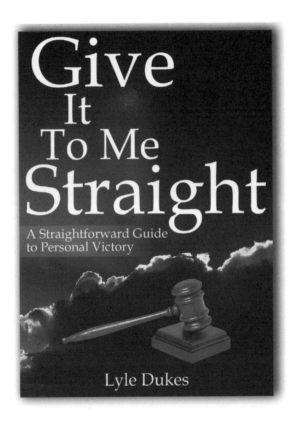

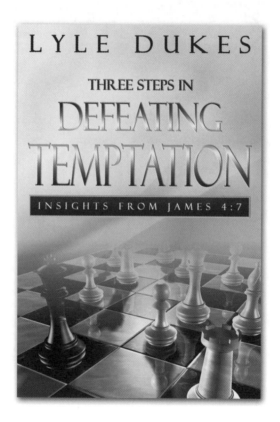

Harvest Life Changers Church, International Mass Choir

He's Right There

Live

Order this soul-stirring CD by phone or online!

8-PSTOR-DUKES
(877) 867-3853

www.lyleanddeborahdukes.com

To request a Lyle and Deborah Dukes Ministries Product Catalog call us toll free or write to Lyle and Deborah Dukes Ministries, P.O. Box 431, Woodbridge, Virginia 22194

COME VISIT THE HARVEST!

HARVEST LIFE CHANGERS CHURCH, INTERNATIONAL

14401 TELEGRAPH ROAD . WOODBRIDGE, VIRGINIA 22192

(703) 490-4040

If you are ever in the Woodbridge, Virginia area, we invite you to worship with us during our Sunday services and on Wednesdays for Pastoral Bible Teaching!

SERVICE SCHEDULE

Sunday Services

8:00 am......9:00 am......11:30 am

Youth Church is available during the 11:30 am service (Pre-K3 - Grade 5)

Wednesday

Intercessory Prayer............7:00 pm

Pastoral Bible Teaching....7:30 pm

Youth Ministry...................7:30 pm

(Grade 6-12)

Directions: From I-95, take exit 158B (Prince William Pkwy) toward Manassas. Turn left onto Telegraph Road. Follow the road three quarters of a mile and look for the Potomac Mills highway sign on the left. Harvest Life Changers Church is located at 14401 Telegraph Road, behind IKEA.

All are welcome!

PASTOR LYLE DUKES & CO-PASTOR DEBORAH DUKES

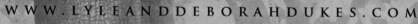